ADVENTURES IN ANCIENT EGYPT

This book is for my daughter, Lia Grainger, who once did a school project
on the Sphinx and has been in love with all things Egyptian ever since.
L.B.

For Phil and Rosemary, who inspire me with their
love of travel to exotic places.
B.S.

Acknowledgements

I am extremely grateful for the help of Dr Julie Anderson of the Department of
Near Eastern and Asian Civilizations, Royal Ontario Museum. She reviewed the manuscript
for accuracy, cheerfully and knowledgeably answered even the most arcane questions, and
provided ongoing and invaluable advice. Any errors or inaccuracies in the text are my own.

Many thanks to Valerie Wyatt, my editor, whose fine mind and fun-loving spirit
made this book's evolution a pleasure. Thanks also to Bill Slavin for bringing the Binkertons
so splendidly to life on the page, and to Julia Naimska for her care with the book's design.

My friend and fellow writer, Deborah Hodge, has been a wise and much-appreciated reader
of Binkerton manuscripts for years. I am also grateful for the feedback of Emily McLellan and
Jeremie Lauck Stephenson, the book's first age-appropriate readers.

My family provided laughs, ideas, support and a happy environment in which to create.
Thank you, Bill, Lia and Tess. My friend Anna Koeller provided critiques, great food and dog-walking.
Finally, I would like to thank Mr Visch, my high school history teacher – he made it fun!

This edition published 2000 in Great Britain by
A & C Black (Publishers) Ltd, 35 Bedford Row, London WC1R 4JH

First published 2000 in Canada by Kids Can Press Ltd

Edited by Valerie Wyatt
Designed by Julia Naimska
Printed in Hong Kong

ISBN 0-7136-5758-8

A CIP catalogue record for this book is available from the British Library.

ADVENTURES IN
ANCIENT
EGYPT

Adventures? Huh! It's tough and scary.

It's hot and sweaty.

It's... fun!

Written by Linda Bailey
Illustrated by Bill Slavin

A & C Black · London

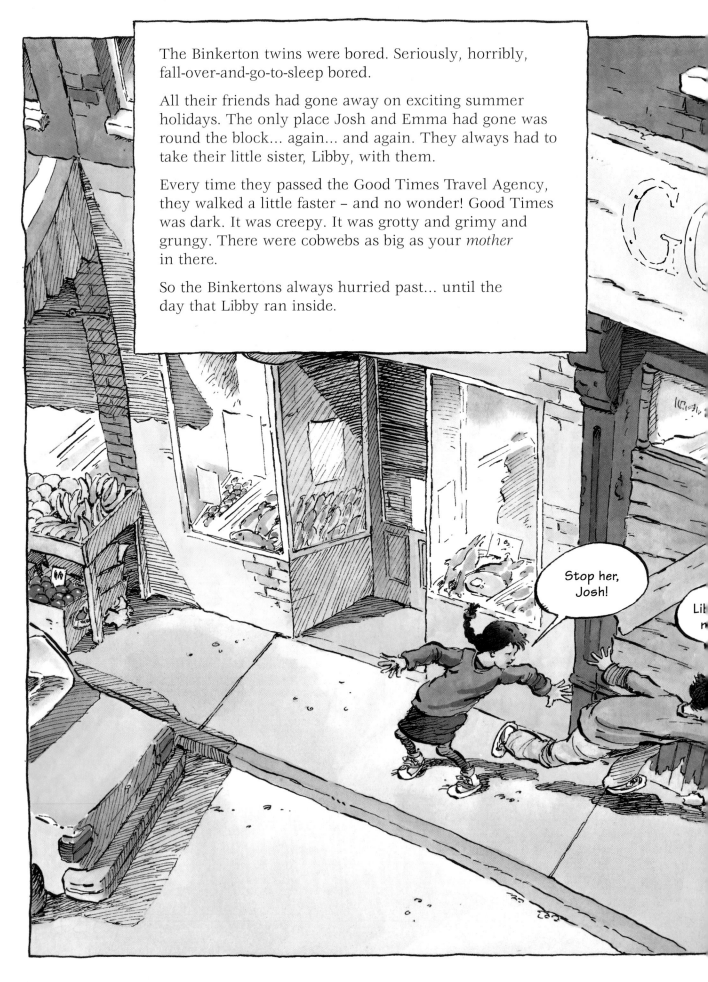

The Binkerton twins were bored. Seriously, horribly, fall-over-and-go-to-sleep bored.

All their friends had gone away on exciting summer holidays. The only place Josh and Emma had gone was round the block... again... and again. They always had to take their little sister, Libby, with them.

Every time they passed the Good Times Travel Agency, they walked a little faster – and no wonder! Good Times was dark. It was creepy. It was grotty and grimy and grungy. There were cobwebs as big as your *mother* in there.

So the Binkertons always hurried past... until the day that Libby ran inside.

If it had been up to Emma, the Binkertons would have been out of there in two seconds flat. But Libby, as usual, made things difficult.

Oh my! We haven't had a customer since...

1918? 1981? 1819?

We're not customers, we're —

Good kitty.

Ow! LIB-BEE!!

1934

Wright Bros. TOURS

The more Emma saw of the travel agency, and the more she heard from Mr Pettigrew, the more nervous she became.

What a weird old book.

Ancient Egypt? Excellent choice! You'll love it there!

Love it where? What do you mean?

Even though Emma had never seen Mr Pettigrew's weird old book before, she had a very strange feeling about it – so strange that she tried to keep her brother from opening it. She *almost* succeeded.

Josh! Don't!

Julian T. Pettigrew's Personal Guide to

ANCIENT EGYPT

*Open this book and your journey's begun.
Read every word and your journey is done.*

But *almost* wasn't quite enough. There was a terrible, wonderful flash and…

Have a good time!

9

...in one brief moment, everything changed!

Wh-what? Where are we?

Oh... my... gosh.

JULIAN T. PETTIGREW'S PERSONAL GUIDE TO ANCIENT EGYPT

WELCOME to ancient Egypt! And congratulations on picking this hot, sunny spot for your holiday. You've chosen a terrific time – around 2500 BC.

Did you bring an umbrella? If so, you can dump it right now. It almost never rains in ancient Egypt. In fact, most of the land around here is desert. The only reason it isn't *all* desert is the Nile River.

Ah... the Nile. What a magnificent river it is! Why? Because without the Nile, nothing else in ancient Egypt would be possible. It flows north from the mountains in Africa through the desert to the sea, providing life-giving water to the land on each side.

It took Emma just a few seconds to work out what had happened – the Binkertons had travelled through time.

We're in ancient Egypt, Josh! It says so right here.

After a careful look at the guidebook, Emma worked out something else. They were stuck there! They couldn't go home until they had read every word of *Julian T. Pettigrew's Personal Guide to Ancient Egypt.*

Well, we wanted a holiday.

Yes, but not 4,500 years away from home!

Imagine an oasis 1,000 km long and only a few kilometres wide, and you'll have a pretty good idea of what ancient Egypt was like. See for yourself on the map. It's the long, skinny green bit.

Mediterranean Sea

Western Desert Nile River

Red Sea

Eastern Desert

It's lucky you turned up at flood time. Every year, between July and October, the Nile overflows its banks and floods the surrounding fields. This is called the Inundation. The people here love it, and so they should. When the river goes down again, it leaves behind a thick layer of fertile mud – great for growing crops of all kinds.

In the meantime, the countryside can get a little... well... damp.

Wading around in the muddy waters of the Nile wasn't going to get the Binkertons anywhere. So they headed for higher ground – and their first real, live Egyptians.

At least, the Binkertons *hoped* they were alive.

She doesn't look 4,500 years old.

My name is Aneksi. Welcome to my home.

ANCIENT EGYPTIAN HOMES

If you want to see a typical Egyptian home, drop in on a farming family. Most ancient Egyptians are peasant-farmers. They live in small villages along the Nile and grow crops in the rich black soil left by the flood. They build their houses on high ground that the flood doesn't reach.

Building a house in ancient Egypt is easy. Even *you* could do it. All you need is mud, and there's plenty of that around. Just mix it with straw and put it into moulds.

Leave it to bake in the sun and, hey presto – mud bricks! The Egyptians plaster these bricks together to make houses. The flat roofs are used as extra living space. The windows are high and small to keep the house cool. Some houses are painted white inside and out.

The houses of ordinary people are small and don't have a lot of furniture – just a few stools or small tables and mats. Wood is scarce here, so wooden furniture is expensive.

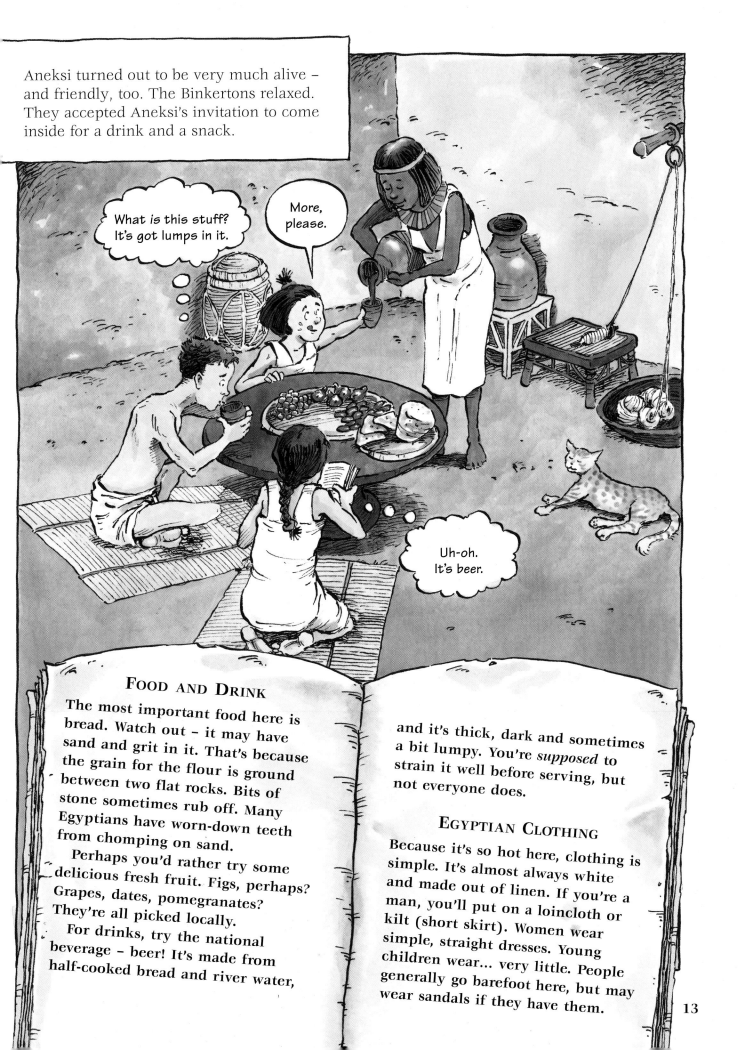

Aneksi turned out to be very much alive – and friendly, too. The Binkertons relaxed. They accepted Aneksi's invitation to come inside for a drink and a snack.

What *is* this stuff? It's got lumps in it.

More, please.

Uh-oh. It's beer.

FOOD AND DRINK

The most important food here is bread. Watch out – it may have sand and grit in it. That's because the grain for the flour is ground between two flat rocks. Bits of stone sometimes rub off. Many Egyptians have worn-down teeth from chomping on sand.

Perhaps you'd rather try some delicious fresh fruit. Figs, perhaps? Grapes, dates, pomegranates? They're all picked locally.

For drinks, try the national beverage – beer! It's made from half-cooked bread and river water, and it's thick, dark and sometimes a bit lumpy. You're *supposed* to strain it well before serving, but not everyone does.

EGYPTIAN CLOTHING

Because it's so hot here, clothing is simple. It's almost always white and made out of linen. If you're a man, you'll put on a loincloth or kilt (short skirt). Women wear simple, straight dresses. Young children wear... very little. People generally go barefoot here, but may wear sandals if they have them.

Just as Emma was trying to think of a polite way to say that they didn't drink beer, a group of official-looking men arrived. They had come to get Aneksi's brother, Hapu, to take him to work for the king.

But Hapu wasn't there – and Josh was! Josh tried to explain that they'd got the wrong boy...

Come along quietly, Hapu.

You're making a mistake! I'm – HELP! EMMA!

But we don't even *live* here.

ANCIENT EGYPTIAN SOCIETY

If you had to pick a job in ancient Egypt, a good choice would be king. The king owns all the land. He owns everything in it. He runs the country and everyone obeys his commands without question. To the ancient Egyptians, he isn't just a king – he's also a living god. The people here believe he's the son of Re (or Ra), their sun god. They believe he can speak directly to the gods and ask for good floods and rich crops.

Other jobs in ancient Egypt aren't quite as good as king. Below him are the nobles and officials, who help him rule. Below them are the temple priests and scribes, who are respected because they can read and write. A step lower are the skilled craftsmen. Down at the bottom are the farmers and labourers. Most people in ancient Egypt are at the bottom of the society – where there's plenty of room!

14

Emma felt sick. Josh wasn't perfect – far from it – but he was the only brother she had! She and Libby set out after him. Eventually, they came to a bustling settlement beside the Nile. Emma was positive they would find Josh there.

We'll find him if we have to take this town apart, brick by brick.

Find-Joshy, find-Joshy, find –

Over the next few hours, the two girls dragged themselves from one end of town to another, searching for their brother. They knocked on doors and stopped strangers in the street. They questioned craftsmen selling their wares.

Joshy?

He has brown eyes and – no, I have some sandals at home, thank you!

AN EGYPTIAN TOWN

Try to spend at least some of your holiday in one of the larger towns along the Nile. Towns are centres of trade and government. They're also great places for people-watching. The streets, especially in the poorer sections, are narrow and crowded with people going about their business. If you feel like shopping, look for craftsmen selling pottery, sandals, reed mats and other products.

Notice a nasty smell or two? Try to ignore it. There's no rubbish collection here and no sewer system, and what with the heat...

They spoke to priests at a temple.

He's about this tall and –

Out! Out!

TEMPLES AND GODS

Religious temples are quiet and peaceful, but don't expect to be invited inside. An Egyptian temple is like a private palace for a god to live in. The god is represented by a statue, kept in a shrine. The statue is washed, dressed and even fed by temple priests. It doesn't actually *eat* the food, of course. (Fortunately, the priests have good appetites.)

The ancient Egyptians believe in hundreds of different gods. Not all have great temples. Some are worshipped only in certain parts of the country. Others are household spirits thought to help with everyday problems. Many Egyptian gods are shown in animal form, for example the crocodile, the hawk, the lion and the hippopotamus.

17

Hour after hour, Emma and Libby searched, while the hot Egyptian sun beat down on their backs. By the end of the day, the girls were tired, hungry and parched with thirst.

Perfect. Sunburnt, too.

Pssst! Want a job?

When they were offered food and lodging – in exchange for work – they had no choice but to accept. A wealthy family that was giving a party was short of servants. Emma was a little shocked by the party entertainment...

Oh dear. Don't look, Libby!

Wow!

...but Libby leapt right in.

Hey, Emma! Watch me.

I am *never* taking her anywhere again!

A BANQUET

If you're hanging around with wealthy Egyptians, you may be invited to a banquet. Don't be shy. Put some flowers round your neck and join in the fun!

The food's terrific. There's roast goose, duck and quail served with fresh vegetables – onions, leeks, beans, cucumbers and lettuce. And lucky you! Beef is on the menu. Only wealthy people can afford this luxury. If you have a sweet tooth, look for honey cakes, figs and other fresh fruit. For drinks, most guests wash their food down with wine – sometimes too *much* wine.

Don't forget your table manners. Squat or sit close to the table. Sit with the men if you're male, or the women if you're female. Use your fingers to eat – but not all of them! Only use three fingers of your right hand.

The best part of a banquet is the entertainment. The ancient Egyptians adore music. Feel free to clap along with the flutes, harps, drums, rattles – and dancing girls! The dancers twist and bend like gymnasts. They even do acrobatic stunts. (Perhaps it helps that they don't wear too many clothes.)

Finished eating? Try a game of senet. It's a quiet board game which is very popular here.

19

Over the next few days, Emma and Libby continued to work for the Egyptian family while spending every spare moment searching for Josh. When one of the other servants told them about a teacher 'who knows many things,' they tracked down the man at his school.

It is true, I know many things.

L-I-B-B-Y. Libby!

Unfortunately, the teacher didn't know the one thing that mattered to Emma and Libby.

...and after the great King Djoser came Sekhemkhet and Khaba, followed by the long reign of King Huni and...

Where's the off button?

C-A-T. Cat!

Emma had one uncomfortable moment when the teacher noticed the guidebook and wanted a closer look. But she quickly distracted him by asking about *his* books.

That's a book?

...and in the reign of the great King Sneferu, in the time of the flood...

I-J-I-P-T. Egypt!

Help!

Mrowp!

LEARNING AND SCHOOLS

Most learning goes on at home. Boys learn the same work as their fathers – fishing, farming, craftwork and so on. Girls are taught to run a household by their mothers.

Some boys (and a few privileged girls) are taught reading, writing and maths in small schools. Warning: if you visit a school, be careful near the teacher – especially if he has a big stick in his hand! There's an old Egyptian saying: 'A boy's ears are on his back. He listens best when he is beaten.'

Some hard-working boys become scribes (men trained to write letters, record information and help run the government). Scribes can become priests or army officers – or even prime minister. It's a great honour to be a scribe – and easier than doing farmwork in the hot sun!

Perhaps you'd like to learn the ancient Egyptian alphabet while you're here. How hard can it be? Well... quite hard, actually. It's a kind of picture-writing called hieroglyphics, and it has more than 700 different symbols.

To try it, you'll need a reed brush and some ink made from soot. Practise on bits of broken pottery (ostraca). Scrolls of paper (papyrus) are made from thin strips of reeds pounded together. But they're *much* too precious to waste on students.

21

As time passed with no word of Josh, Emma grew more and more anxious. At night, she lay awake worrying.

How will I ever explain to Mum and Dad?

She worried in the daytime, too – mostly about how to keep her sister out of trouble!

LIB-BEE! What are you doing?

SLEEPING IN ANCIENT EGYPT

Rich Egyptians sleep on wooden-framed beds. Poorer people sleep on mats or on clay platforms covered in matting. To beat the heat, you may want to bed down, Egyptian-style, on the roof. Aaah… feel that breeze? Nice and cool!

Looking for a pillow? Try an ancient Egyptian headrest. They're made of wood, ivory or stone, and they *look* like instruments of torture. They can come in handy, though, for keeping your head off the ground – especially when scorpions or snakes wander by.

MAKE-UP AND JEWELLERY

If you want to look your best in Egypt, make-up is just the thing. First, outline your eyes with black kohl and green eye paint. Stain your fingernails with henna. Dab yourself with scented oils. (In ancient Egypt, it's important to smell nice.)

Next put on jewellery – coloured beads perhaps, or a gold bracelet or amulet (magic charm) to ward off evil spirits. Finish your new look with a wig. People here keep their hair short and wear wigs on special occasions.

There! You're gorgeous.

Libby quickly made friends with the local children. She fitted in well – in Emma's opinion, a little *too* well.

Put your clothes back on, Libby!

WHYYYY?

One day, Libby and her new friends went off to swim in the river. Emma was relieved... until she read the next page in the guidebook.

Crocodiles? In the Nile? Oh no... LIBBY!

EGYPTIAN CHILDREN

Young children in ancient Egypt wear very few clothes. Actually... none. After all, it *is* very hot. You may notice an odd hairstyle, called a 'lock of youth', on the boys. They wear it until they're ten or twelve.

Egyptian children have simple home-made dolls, tops and wheeled toys. They love to wrestle and play tug-of-war and ball games. Also, living beside the Nile, they like to go swimming. It's a shame there are crocodiles. But don't worry. Only a *few* children get eaten.

Running as hard as she could, Emma managed – only just – to snatch her little sister from the jaws of death.

Here, boy.

LIB-BEEE! NO!

Emma collapsed, exhausted, on the river bank. That's where she noticed the boats.

Maybe someone here has seen him!

Joshy?

HUNTING AND FISHING

The Nile is full of food – if you can catch it! Try fishing with spears or nets, or hooks and lines. You could also go after some of the waterfowl that live in the marshy areas – ducks, geese, herons or cranes. Ancient Egyptians trap these birds in nets or use throw-sticks to bring them down.

If you feel like taking your life in your hands, you could try hippo-hunting. Join some other hunters in a small boat and sneak up on a huge hippopotamus. Throw a spear at it. Bear in mind that the hippopotamus will *not* like this!

On second thoughts, forget hippo-hunting.

Walking along the river bank, the girls finally got a lucky break. Some men building a papyrus boat had seen Josh only two days before.

The problem now was how to travel down the Nile. But watching the men had given Emma an idea. Why couldn't she and Libby build their own boat?

TRAVEL ON THE NILE
The Nile is Egypt's great highway. All you need is a boat! If you want to go north, just drift with the current. To go south, put up a sail and let the wind carry you. (Paddles and poles help, too.) Watch out for other boats – fishing boats, cargo boats, pleasure boats and huge barges. Most common of all are small boats made from papyrus reeds.

HOW TO BUILD A PAPYRUS BOAT
Cut down some papyrus reeds. (You'll find them growing beside the river.) Lash them together in bundles. Tie them tightly, or they won't be waterproof. Now make the ends point upwards. Ready? Away you go!
(P.S. You *can* swim, can't you?)

As Emma and Libby floated down the great Egyptian highway, they saw their first pyramids. Not all of them were perfect.

Well, it's a start.

Better.

Bingo!

PYRAMIDS

If there's one thing you *must* see in ancient Egypt, it's the pyramids.

They're huge! They're awesome! And they're built with just one purpose – as tombs for Egyptian kings. The ancient Egyptians believe that the king lives on after death. But he can only do this if his soul (Ba) and his life force (Ka) can return to his dead body when they need to. That's why, when a king dies, his body is preserved in a life-like condition and placed in a burial chamber deep inside or beneath a pyramid.

It took the Egyptians a few generations to work out how to build pyramids.

At first, they just put the king's body in a mastaba (a rectangle made of mud bricks with a burial chamber underneath).

Then they piled up a few mastabas to make a step pyramid with six 'steps'.

Meanwhile, further down the Nile, Josh had been given a very big job. In fact, in the whole history of the family, no Binkerton had *ever* been given such a huge job.

Okay, Mr Pettigrew, joke's over. Can I go home now?

After that came a bent pyramid. This was *almost* right.

Finally... success! A true pyramid shape.

Next, the Egyptians decided to make some really *big* pyramids. How big? Would you believe as tall as a forty-storey skyscraper? Would you believe more than 2 million limestone blocks? Would you believe over 6 million tons of rock? That's big!

Imagine building something that huge with no machinery. No bulldozers, no cranes, no wheels – just human muscle! Thousands of workers are needed to do the job – as many as 4,000 all year round, with 20,000 or 30,000 extra during flood season. Even with all those workers, it can take twenty years or more to build a pyramid.

What does all this mean to you? Well, if you are 'volunteered' to help, you could be here for a *long* time.

How to Build a Pyramid
(just in case they put you in charge)

1. Pick a good spot – on the west side of the Nile, above the flood line and close to a large deposit of limestone.
2. Make the spot level. Then mark out the four sides of the pyramid to face north, south, east and west.
3. Quarry the limestone – cut large blocks out of the ground, using simple tools made of copper, wood or stone.
4. Take the limestone blocks to the spot you picked. (Hint: this is the hard part.) Put ropes around them and drag them on sledges. Use logs with oil or water to make a good sliding path. (Blocks from far away will have to be dragged to the river, floated on a barge and *then* dragged to the site.)

5. Build the pyramid. (Hint: this is the *really* hard part.) After you've made the first layer of stone, you will have to build ramps so that you can drag the heavy blocks... uphill!
6. Keep building. Keep building. Keep building. Keep building.
7. Oops! Did you remember to dig a burial chamber underneath the pyramid first? Did you leave space for a passage to the chamber?
8. Put a special pyramid-shaped stone (a cap stone) on top.
9. Smooth and polish the shiny white limestone on the outside so the pyramid will gleam in the sun.
10. Take down the ramps. Isn't it lovely? Aren't you proud?

Like the other pyramid workers, Josh was getting paid for his work. But he wasn't impressed with the wages.

He complained to his fellow workers, but they weren't very sympathetic.

Onions? I'm killing myself for onions?

It is our duty to build the king's tomb.

He will look after us in the afterlife.

We are the Strong Gang!

Sigh!

SPECIAL TIPS FOR PYRAMID WORKERS

* Watch out for heatstroke!
* Watch out for insects!
* Don't get sunburnt!
* Avoid rope burn!
* Drink plenty of water!
* Try not to get crushed!

* Don't fall off the pyramid!
* BE CAREFUL!

Phew! If you make it through the day, you can go and collect your wages – bread, beer, onions and clothing. Have fun!

He also tried to get a different job. The craftsmen's jobs looked much easier, so Josh asked if he could swap.

It was very discouraging.

Fortunately, help was on its way. That night, as the pyramid workers slept, Emma and Libby crept silently into their sleeping quarters. At least, that was the *plan*.

JOSHY! HI! WAKE UP, JOSHY!

The Binkertons were so thrilled to be together again, they were speechless.

They headed for the papyrus boat that the girls had hidden in the reeds. They were almost there when Libby spotted a pyramid with an open entrance.

Libby, no!

Stop her, Josh!

Sightseeing in the middle of a getaway? This was a *very* bad idea. Emma and Josh tried to lure their little sister out of the pyramid.

Yoo-hoo, Libby! Would you like a nice juicy fig?

I'll give you a piggyback ride, Libby.

CITY OF THE DEAD

You have probably already noticed that a pyramid doesn't just sit out in the desert all by itself – it's surrounded by a whole pyramid complex. This includes:

1. A valley temple where the dead king's body is received when it is brought here by boat.
2. A causeway (covered road) between the valley temple and the mortuary temple.
3. A mortuary temple where funeral services are performed and where food and other offerings are made.
4. A low wall around the base of the pyramid.
5. Small pyramids for the king's wives (sometimes).
6. Rows of mastabas where the king's family and special friends are buried after they die.

The main pyramid, the smaller pyramids and the mastabas are all tombs (graves). Together, they make up a City of the Dead.

It's a nice place for a tourist like you to visit... but you wouldn't want to live there!

But Libby had disappeared. Emma and Josh had to follow her... into the pitch-black tunnel.

③

②

①

INSIDE A PYRAMID

If you could see right through a pyramid, you'd find that it's mostly (but not all) solid stone. Here are some of the things you might see:

1. The core blocks on the inside. They're made of ordinary limestone. Because they're hidden underneath, they don't have to fit together perfectly.

2. The packing blocks, resting on the core blocks.

3. The casing blocks on the outside. These are made of special white limestone. They're fitted together so tightly that you can't even poke a hair between them.

4. The entrance to the pyramid on its north face.

5. A passage leading from the entrance to the burial chamber.

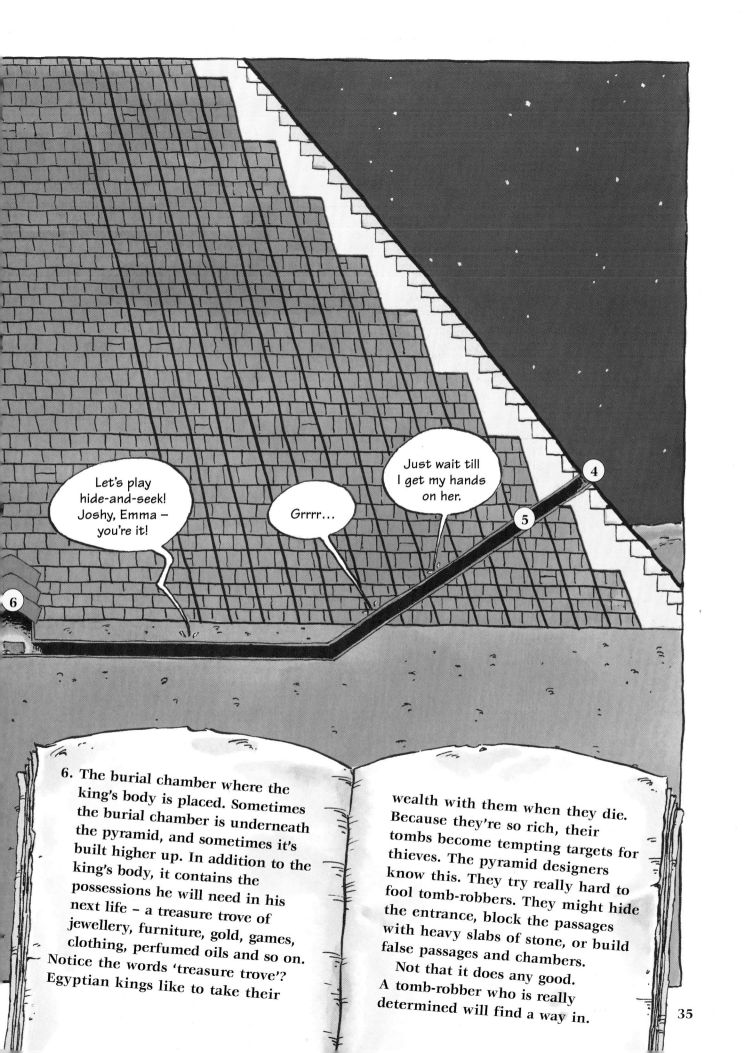

Let's play hide-and-seek! Joshy, Emma – you're it!

Grrrr...

Just wait till I get my hands on her.

6. The burial chamber where the king's body is placed. Sometimes the burial chamber is underneath the pyramid, and sometimes it's built higher up. In addition to the king's body, it contains the possessions he will need in his next life – a treasure trove of jewellery, furniture, gold, games, clothing, perfumed oils and so on. Notice the words 'treasure trove'? Egyptian kings like to take their wealth with them when they die. Because they're so rich, their tombs become tempting targets for thieves. The pyramid designers know this. They try really hard to fool tomb-robbers. They might hide the entrance, block the passages with heavy slabs of stone, or build false passages and chambers.

Not that it does any good. A tomb-robber who is really determined will find a way in.

35

3. Remove the stomach, liver, lungs and intestines. Store them in special jars.
4. Leave the heart inside the body. The ancient Egyptians believe that the heart is where all thought and feeling happen.
5. Cover the body in a special drying powder called natron. Let it dry for forty days or so.
6. The dried-out body will have loose skin. Stuff it with padding (clay, straw, sawdust or linen) to fill it out.
7. Put sweet-smelling oils and ointments on the body.
8. Wrap the body in linen strips soaked in resin (a substance that comes from trees). You will need hundreds of metres of these strips. Put jewels, gold and amulets in between the layers.
9. The mummy is finished. It is ready to be put in a sarcophagus (stone coffin) in its tomb, where it will stay forever... or will it?
10. Watch out for tomb-robbers!

The Binkertons had really done it this time. They'd arrived in the tomb just hours after it had been robbed – and minutes before the king's guards showed up!

Once again, all the Binkertons' explanations were ignored.

Josh tried to find out what would happen to them next.

What's the penalty for tomb-robbing?

Impalement.

I was hoping it might be detention.

TOMB-ROBBERS

There is one group of people in ancient Egypt whom you should avoid at all costs. STAY AWAY FROM TOMB-ROBBERS! Stay away from opened tombs and pyramids, too. They're nothing but trouble.

How will you know when you meet a tomb-robber? Here are a few clues. Any greedy treasure-hunter can try to rob a tomb, but certain people have a better chance of succeeding. For example, the people who help to *build* a pyramid (and know about passages and so on) may come back later to rob it.

Pyramid guards sometimes let their robber pals inside – for a price. Even temple officials can be tempted to steal the fabulous riches inside a pyramid.

So keep your eyes wide open, and steer clear of anyone who even *looks* like a tomb-robber. Remember, there are serious penalties for tomb-robbing in ancient Egypt. You could be impaled on a stake. In case you're not sure what this means, let me explain: THEY WILL THROW YOU ON TO A SHARP STICK! Serious enough for you?

39

At the entrance to the pyramid, the party ran into a second group of guards trying to come inside. This was the Binkertons' chance to escape!

They didn't stop running until they reached the boat.

For the rest of the night, the Binkertons travelled along the Nile. To help his sisters stay awake, Josh told Egyptian jokes.

What does an Egyptian queen eat? Cleo-pasta!

Groan...

They reached the town just as the sun rose. Emma was eager to finish reading the guidebook so that they could go home.

Here, kitty!

Mrowp?

Good! Light enough to read.

Unfortunately for the Binkertons, they weren't the only ones who had spent the night in a boat. The guards had reached the town ahead of them!

Reading while you run is generally a very bad idea – unless, of course, your life depends on it!

Emma's eyes flew over the pages as quickly as her legs flew over the ground. It was a lot to handle at the same time. In fact, it was too much.

Now Josh wasn't the bravest person in all of ancient Egypt – nor the strongest, nor the brainiest. But he was a Binkerton. And if there's one thing a Binkerton is, it's loyal. Seeing his sister fall, he skidded to a halt.

The Binkertons ran as hard and as fast as they could...

...but in the end...

Faster, Josh! Read faster!

And-now-as-your-holiday-in-ancient-Egypt-draws-to-a-close...

SAY GOODBYE

And now, as your holiday in ancient Egypt draws to a close, you probably have many fond memories of the fascinating people you have met and the marvellous things you have seen.

Before you leave, why not take the time for a final stroll through town? If you have any last-minute shopping to do, here's your chance. Or maybe you'd rather just relax and enjoy a last peaceful moment in this sun-blessed land. Close your eyes, soak up the rays... and breathe in the scent of the flowers. Then it will be time to say a final goodbye to the soft, warm days and lovely, cool nights of this fabled civilisation. It is an experience you will never forget for the rest of your lives.

The End

44

...they couldn't run fast enough.

Their only chance was to *read* fast enough! Fast enough to finish the book and get –

...but Emma and Libby just wanted to see their parents.

I want to go home!

Me too, Lib.

As the Binkertons left the Good Times Travel Agency, they swore they would never come near the place again.

Don't be strangers!

I'm not even walking round this *block* again!

But *never?* Well, that's a very long time.

Even for time travellers.

Julian T. Pettigrew's Personal Guide to the MIDDLE AGES

Open this boo
your journe
Read eve
your

ANCIENT EGYPT

Fact or fantasy?

How much can you believe of *Adventures in Ancient Egypt*? The story of the Binkertons and their adventures is just that – a story. However, all the information in *Julian T. Pettigrew's Personal Guide to Ancient Egypt* is based on things that we know really happened in ancient Egypt – in other words, historical fact.

More about ancient Egypt

How ancient was it? Very! The civilisation that we call 'ancient Egypt' began more than 5,000 years ago (around 3100 BC) and lasted for more than 3,000 years. It grew up in the Nile Valley in northern Africa. Why there? Well, the climate was sunny, and the Nile River provided a good life – rich soil, plenty of water and a useful means of transport. It was a place where people could grow crops and organise communities.

There were three important periods in ancient Egypt – the Old Kingdom, the Middle Kingdom and the New Kingdom. The Binkertons' story is set around 2500 BC, during the Old Kingdom (2686 BC to 2181 BC). This was the time when the great stone pyramids were built. It is sometimes called 'the Pyramid Age'. Pyramids were also built in the Middle Kingdom, but they didn't last as long. In the New Kingdom, the Egyptians buried their rulers in secret tombs in the Valley of the Kings (although we usually call the kings of this time 'pharaohs').

But back to the Old Kingdom. No one knows exactly how the pyramids were built. Some remains of long, straight ramps have been found. So experts are pretty sure ramps were used, but they can't agree on how or what kind.

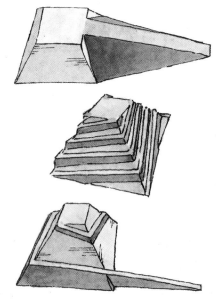

Did they use a single ramp to build the pyramids?

Did they use four ramps that wrapped around the pyramid, like the one Josh worked on?

Did they use single *and* wrap-around ramps? No one really knows.

In fact, we don't really know about a *lot* of things in ancient Egypt. For example, when the Binkertons were accused of tomb-robbing, they were threatened with impalement (being thrown on to a sharp stick). There is evidence that impalement was used as a punishment later in ancient Egypt, but we're not sure about in the Old Kingdom. Egyptologists (people who study ancient Egypt) are still learning about this ancient culture.

Amazing discoveries have been made which help us to find out more. One of the most important was the Rosetta Stone, which was found by a French soldier in 1799. This flat stone has the same information carved on it in three different languages – ancient Egyptian hieroglyphics, a later form of Egyptian writing, and ancient Greek. Before it was found, people had no way of understanding hieroglyphics. The Rosetta Stone broke the code, solving many of the mysteries of ancient Egypt.